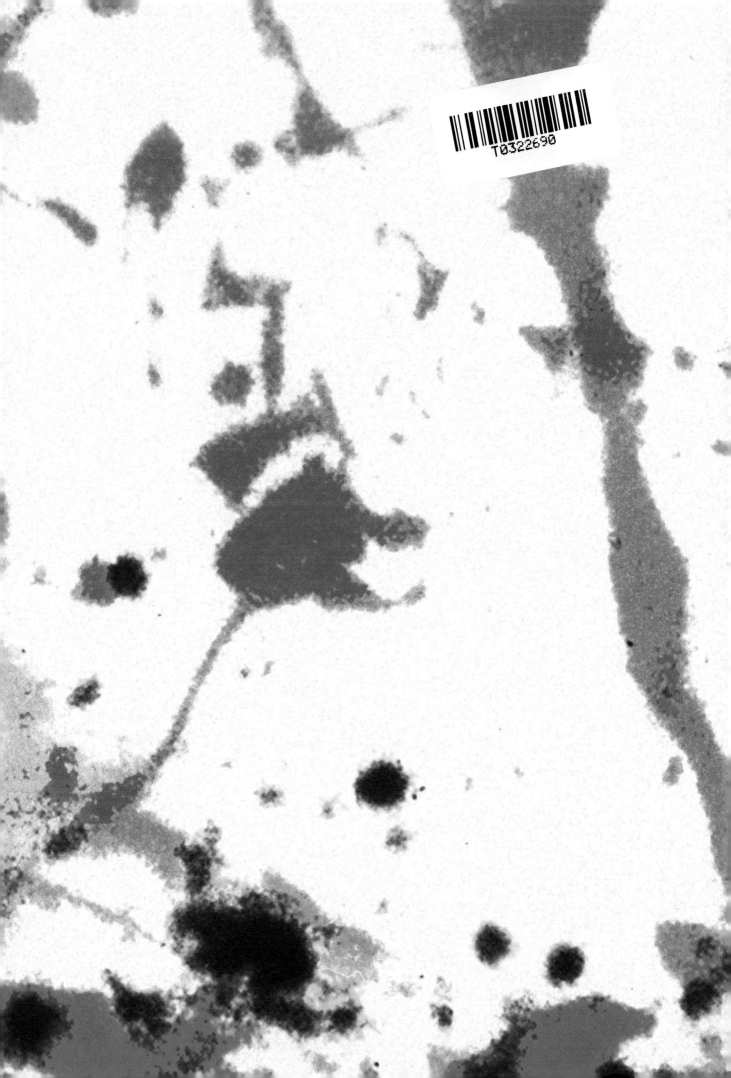

YOUNG PUNKS

SHEILA ROCK

When Sheila Rock was taking the bulk of the photographs in this book, I was looking at Punk from the perspective of editor of the *NME*. What Sheila saw and photographed was what made it a dynamic and exciting period for me too: the attitude and energy of Punk was a gift to music journalism after the dreariness of much early Seventies rock music, glam rock excepted.

I met her first, post-*NME*, when I was launch editor of *Smash Hits*, and our working relationship thrived with the launch of *The Face* in 1980. More than most, Sheila very quickly understood what I was trying to achieve: a modern, photo-journal of record where 'the look' counted for as much as the music.

To put it into historical context, the term 'youth culture' had yet to be coined. As a magazine, there was no existing template for *The Face* to follow, and the long-term ambition of the magazine was fluid at best. Evolving month by month, we were breaking new ground and learning on the job: me as independent publisher/editor, Neville Brody as art director, and Sheila as photographer.

Sheila shot three of the first ten covers, but her major contribution was to challenge the magazine's editorial scope. Always self-effacing but sweetly persuasive, she'd appear in the office with a series of unsolicited shoots that featured a small coterie of musicians showing off clothes that fitted their personalities – Ranking Roger in a zoot suit, John Cooper Clarke as Regency beau – until the pretext of incorporating musicians for credibility alone gave way to spreads that made no apologies for being about clothes and attitude. We had stumbled into fashion.

Pushed to accommodate material unexpected in what was then regarded as a rock magazine, we came up with the term 'style' as a label for these spreads, deeming the alternative 'fashion' to be a turn-off. As a result, when the mainstream press began to take notice of *The Face*, 'style magazine' was the genre ascribed to us.

In short, Sheila's exploration paved the way for *The Face* to become the vehicle that stylist Ray Petri chose to launch his career, and later brought the likes of Juergen Teller, Albert Watson, Mario Testino and Corinne Day to our door.

The qualities she brought to *The Face* are there in these photos from earlier in her career. Sheila didn't wait around for a commission. Recognising the import of the changes she was witnessing, Sheila Rock used her camera as an enthusiastic observer to document the explosion of youth culture that foreshadowed what we see around us today.

Nick Logan

CONVERSATION

Sheila Rock
Young Punks is one of many chapters in my story. It's a document of an extraordinary time. Funny what you can find in a shed at the end of the garden. These photographs sat dormant in a box for years and until they were laid out in this coherent way, I didn't realise what an interesting moment in history I had recorded.

Paul Simonon
This book is a great visual history of places, situations and clubs, as well as unknown people on the street. They were inspired by music, wanted to dress in a particular way and to do it or make it themselves.

Jah Wobble
These photos really capture the zeitgeist of that time.

Sheila Rock
I didn't have a clue what I was doing, like all of us. We picked things up to survive. I picked up a camera and just gave it a go. We reinvented ourselves.

Don Letts
When I knew you then, Sheila, you were a photographer. You were tapped into the vibe. And the thing about Punk that people forget was that it wasn't just music. The reason it has the legacy that it does is because it inspired people to make clothes, become graphic artists, photographers, writers and journalists. It was very much a complete subculture. Nothing since has had that complete impact. But Punk kind of painted itself into a box by having a definition. It was never about that – it was about freedom and being able to embrace all these things. The post-Punk period just threw off those shackles.

Jon Savage
Punk denied absolutely everything and cut off its nose to spite its face so it was actually quite hard for things to grow.

Sheila Rock
But, concurrently, it was a time of experimentation, electricity, creativity – it had a sort of dark light.

Jon Savage
We take that for granted now but it enabled a lot of us to do what we wanted to do. I wouldn't necessarily have been able to become a writer without what the Sex Pistols did. It was like plugging yourself into an electric socket – this incredible blast of energy.

Sheila Rock
Wasn't that the same for many of us? We had enthusiasm, we had an inclination, we didn't really know what we were doing but it was like a wave – we were being swept away.

Jon Savage

We are still talking about it 35 years later because it was so complicated and so all-involving and very deep. Profound psychologically in some ways. It was certainly a very profound statement about Britain and what it was to be British and particularly English.

Sheila Rock

When I came to this country, I thought popular music went hand-in-hand with British fashion and was even inspired by it. It was like a marriage. It was tribal – fashion tribes. Because there was no money, people expressed their creativity in the way they dressed.

Jeannette Lee

When I was 16, I was doing my best to dress differently to everyone in my school. I had to really do some research to find the things that made me feel really different. It's even harder to be different now.

Paul Simonon

The pictures in the last chapter show how things started to evolve from Punk; develop and branch out into other areas. How British fashion and history were changing. It's not just about the bands, it's about people... People and their looks.

Jon Savage

If you look at Punk it's all about what's been repressed in English society coming up to the surface. All the ugliness, the excitement, the glee, the taking the piss – all that stuff. Where would we be without it?

Tony James

So many generations believe they've sparked off a cultural revolution but Punks, for the first time, were able to make their own music and records outside of the established record business.

John Krivine

The music was outstanding, the fashion was brilliant, yet the most interesting aspect was Malcolm's [McLaren] political bit. He staged an old fashioned political uprising. He deposed the Royal Family, fermented indecent behavior and indecent apparel, broke a good number of laws, looted the bank of popular culture, raped and pillaged the TV viewing public and he did it all within walking distance of two military barracks (Knightsbridge and Chelsea), almost daring the soldiers to mount up and take to the streets.

Chrissie Hynde

The legacy of Punk is fashion. And fashion is what Punk didn't think it was. It was anti-fashion. It's ironic.

Sheila Rock

At the time I never thought Punk would have the impact or historical significance it has today. When I was photographing, I tried to be attentive to the moment. I was looking for the unusual. Sometimes a mistake. I often find the 'off' moments are the 'best' moments. A successful photograph is often the result of taking a misstep in the right direction...

Paul Simonon

Punk was like stepping stones in the way that one thing would happen and then another thing would happen and it would be overlapping – something would inspire another idea. Constant overlapping and building. It's part of the creative process.

Chrissie Hynde

The word to describe the phenomenon of Punk is non-discrimination. It was telling it like it was – it didn't have any other agenda. The fact that I was a girl didn't matter, it wasn't a novelty. It was my moment.

Jah Wobble

It was OK to be a maverick.

Jeannette Lee

Everybody talks about it now like they knew something really important was happening but I'd be a liar if I said I'd thought everything was changing. It's just with time when you look back you see how important it was.

Steven Severin

You could definitely feel something building all through 1976. More people at shows every week, starting to dress the part. New clubs and shops opening for us. That whole year was so exciting and of course it culminated in the Pistols releasing 'Anarchy' and the floodgates bursting.

Lloyd Johnson

At the time it felt like the early stages of the Mod movement but with different clothes, music and attitude. I felt it as a rebirth of pop culture.

Andy Blade

It was fantastic to be alive; anything and everything was possible. I did honestly feel it was something that would change society for the better, but I was only a kid. Punk gave people like me a chance to get up there and see what they could do.

Rob Symmons

It is amazing, isn't it, what happened? Incredible. People who had nothing could suddenly change everything.

Sheila Rock

It was all about changing and surviving. I think in life you have to try not to be complacent and stuck.

Lloyd Johnson

It's just an evolution. But if I knew then that this was going to be that big, then I'd have learnt to play the guitar!

Jeannette Lee

I think the Seventies were different. It was like the Wild West; all these really interesting characters in fashion and music with no rules. They were doing anything they could to get this thing they love noticed by the public. It was so spontaneous; artistic people who had an itch they just had to scratch.

FASHION

Although grey and overcast and facing a time of economic hardship, something interesting and creative was coming out of Britain.

Punk.

At its core, Punk was an attitude, formed out of a need for self-expression. Young people wanted to set themselves apart and create a sense of identity. This manifested in the unique clothes they wore and the makeup they created; through dressing up and fashion, you could be part of something striking and different. The tribe of Punk emerged.

Punk fashion was provocative: short, spikey hair, paint-splattered clothes, bat-eye makeup, dog collars, razor blades, ripped T-shirts and school uniforms reassembled with safety pins. Black was the colour of choice.

Times were tough and there was little money, but there were a few places in London that sold Punk fashion – if you knew where to find them. Some, like those along the King's Road, Chelsea, were more than just shops: they were gathering places, where those in the know would go to see and to be seen. The shop assistants, through the clothes they wore and the music they played, were mentors and magnets for the people showing up to mingle.

I was drawn to the impact of both the fashion and the music, and how they seamlessly and intrinsically merged. Punk's influence was potent and is still felt across the globe today.

SEX – 1976 (p. 11–19)

Let it Rock – 1971

Too Fast to Live, Too Young to Die – 1972

SEX – 1974 – 1976

Seditionaries – 1977

430 KING'S ROAD, LONDON, SW3

Glen Matlock: I helped make that sign – me and a bloke called Vic. It was plywood with rubber latex and plastic sheeting over the top all stuck together with Bostik [glue]. It was supposed to be like a Rauschenberg.

Jon Savage: I went into SEX several times – it was

Jordan (p. 11–19)

Don Letts: Jordan. To me she was like a character straight out of one of the early John Walters films. She was a trip. You've got to understand she looked like this before Punk really started. That's the thing, Jordan was always really out there. And that was brave.

The shop itself was quite intimidating but that was part of its attraction. It was like an installation and very Eurocentric; it didn't reflect the multicultural way London was heading.

Jon Savage: There are comparatively few shots of the inside of SEX. What's great about these is the level of detail. It was worth buying Malcolm [McLaren] and Vivienne's [Westwood] stuff because it was beautifully designed and they were beautiful objects in the first place.

Acme Attractions – 1974 to 1976 (p. 21 – 25)
135 KING'S ROAD, CHELSEA, SW3
Don Letts and Jeannette Lee – Summer 1976 (p. 25)

Don Letts: The only way people could find this place, as it was literally in the bowels and we didn't have a sign outside, was by word of mouth. Or if you were walking along the road you'd hear bass coming from the basement. It was like a meeting point for all those people who weren't satisfied with the popular culture of the time. All these like-minded rebels, these different tribes, congregated in Acme. Bob Marley would come down there, Patti Smith, Debbie Harry – anybody who was anybody passed through that shop. The Clash, Adverts, Banshees. The Slits used to fucking live down there.

I think people came down for one of three things – the clothes, the music and Jeannette and not necessarily in that order.

Before Punk the soul scene was very big and was in fact the underground alternative for a lot of white kids. Punk was actually the transition from soul.

Acme really was like a club – so cool, I can't tell you. Probably the happiest time of my life: do next-to-fuck-all but look cool, take people's money and meet interesting people.

Jeannette Lee: It was all Don you know, this layout. How good the shop looked. He's got a very artistic eye. He made it really special.

John Krivine: Acme ended in December 1976 because we were asked to leave Antiquarius' basement. We were already getting Punks in the shop in the summer of '76, buying bits and bobs, and they were hearing reggae and rubbing shoulders with black kids their age for the first time because of Don.

BOY – May 1977 (p. 26 – 59)
153 KING'S ROAD, CHELSEA, SW3

Glen Matlock: Malcom [McLaren] had Let It Rock and John [Krivine] had Acme Attractions, and then Malcolm opened SEX and John changed to BOY.

Sheila Rock: John Harwood and Peter Christopherson came up with the concept for BOY. They designed and physically created BOY. They even burnt the walls.

Jon Savage: (p. 28–31) This is the dark side of Punk. You've got the Peter Christopherson cultures of the dead boy in a dish right there probably just before they were raided by the police.

John Krivine: BOY was born in February 1977. The shop's designer was Steph [Stephane Raynor]. He understood Punk fashion perfectly but he could not function in the shadow of the genius at the other end of the road. Then, Peter and John produced a range of T-shirts which were so outrageous that no one would buy them. One of them had a waiver printed on the back saying that if a third party struck the wearer from behind with a blunt instrument, the assailant would not be held accountable in a court of law. We got off to a difficult start but found our niche in the Punk scene by July 1977.

John Krivine – May 1977

Jeannette Lee: He's quite important in my life. If you meet people at the time you are forming ideas, they become significant to you. Forever. People help you on a certain path and you decide to stay on it or not. I think he was very important to `us' actually.
Don Letts: John Krivine – my hat off to this gentleman.

Phil Strongman – May 1977 (opposite)

Jay Strongman – May 1977 (p. 32)

Helen Robinson – February 1977 (p. 51)

Mark Mason – May 1977 (p. 55)

Don Letts: (p. 55) The whole swastika thing was really just young kids lashing out in that kind of naïve way that kids do.

The big
freeze is
on the
way back

By BILL BECKETT

Weather
girl told
'shut up'
on the air

John and Steve, The Photons – 1977 (p. 61 – 63)

Jon Savage: The Photons – Leee Black Childers tried to
manage them because they looked so good.

Beaufort Market – 1977 (p. 64 – 67)

Nigel Pugsley – 1977 (p. 65)

KING'S ROAD, LONDON, SW3

Jon Savage: Beaufort Market – I love the detail. Posters of The Stranglers, Elvis Costello, John Cale – you can see it's already going wrong.

John Krivine: (p. 65) Nigel Pugsley had a shop called Smuts at Beaufort Market just down from SEX.

TRIBE

Faced with widespread unemployment and an economy in tatters, a generation of young people rebelled against the norms of Seventies Britain, creating a movement that fundamentally changed culture and society. The backlash of popular outrage against this seemingly shocking and dangerous phenomenon only increased the appeal.

Being a Punk was more extreme than being a Beat or a Hippie: you had to be brave, ready to stand up to being attacked. Punks were mavericks and outcasts who created their own subculture from top to bottom.

I was struck by how young and innocent everyone was; many Punks were still living at home with their parents. I was a bit older and while I was accepted into the 'tribe' as a photographer, I did not share their rebellion against the system. I felt like a fly on the wall, a shadow in an underground world. The distance created by my camera, my American background and the slight age difference allowed me to roam freely at gigs and events.

Subey – June 1977 (p. 71–72)

Lloyd Johnson: That T-shirt was a knock-off of one from a Frederick's of Hollywood catalogue.

Jah Wobble: At first Punk was stylish but it quickly became a bit 'lowest common denominator'. It became what it wasn't supposed to be: a uniform. Consequently people quickly developed a uniform and, at times, rather thuggish attitude. It had been about not being a conformist.

Jon Savage: (p. 77) That's a classic Punk look – leopard-skin with everyone looking a bit trashy and degraded.

The Stranglers / Cortinas gig – Roundhouse, June 1977 (p. 86–89)

Generation X gig – December 1976 (p. 85)

The Photons – en route to The Stranglers gig, Manchester, October 1977 (above)

The Dictators gig – November 1977 (opposite)

The Jam gig – November 1977 (p. 93)

Alan Drake (opposite)

Magenta Devine, Alan Drake and skinheads (p. 94–95)

Glen Matlock: I remember coming across Magenta for the first time when Iggy played Aylesbury with Bowie on keyboards. Everybody was there. She had silver leather trousers on and everyone went 'Who's that?'

SCENE

Like most underground movements, there was a strong sense of camaraderie in Punk, though there were early factions based around the Sex Pistols and The Clash. In a sense, I aligned myself with the latter: I met The Clash early on, at their gig at the ICA, while I never saw the Sex Pistols play with the original line up.

The close-knit community, and the energy and exposure that came from participating in it, allowed many young people to forge successful careers as artists, writers, designers and filmmakers and, of course, musicians. The raw amateurism was liberating.

Punk was male dominated but it wasn't sexist. Siouxsie Sioux, Debbie Harry, Chrissie Hynde, Poly Styrene, Patti Smith, Viv Albertine, Vivienne Westwood and Jordan are all examples of women who reflected the individuality, self-expression, experimental and risk-taking nature of the moment. I was drawn to their rebellious attitudes, and I found their determination, strength and creativity inspiring.

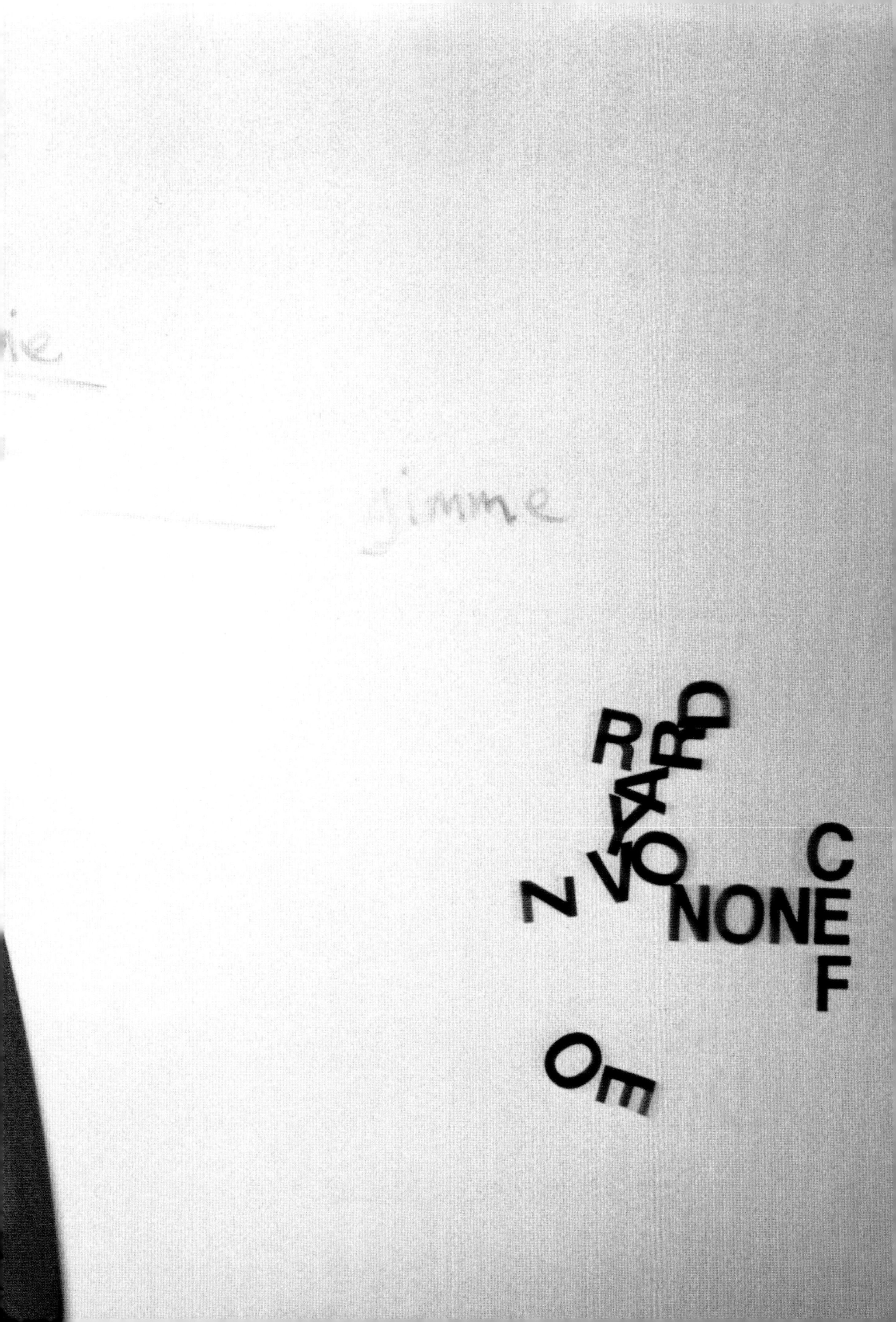

gimme

gimme

R
D
Y
A
N
V
O
NONE
C
E
F
O
E

Jon Savage – December 1977 (opposite and overleaf)
Don Letts – August 1977 (p. 100–101), 1978 (p. 102–103)
Jeannette Lee, Sheila Rock and Don Letts
December 1977 (p. 106)
Poly Styrene – December 1977 (p. 107)

Chris Salewicz: (p. 100) Patti Smith went into Acme Attractions and Don was playing *MPLA*. She asked Don if he knew the man who had made this record. Don knew Tapper Zukie was in London, got in touch with him and got him to appear on stage with Patti Smith. Tapper became part of her entourage. Patti said Tapper was to her like James Brown is to many other people.

Tony James: When we first started, Jon Savage did lots of graphics for Generation X. Designed our posters. He did a lot of those cut-up Constructivist kind of posters.

Jon Savage: (p. 105) I went down to Pollock's in Brixton High Street with Poly Styrene and bought that shirt and also paint-splattered black sta-press. I love that Pollock shirt and I'll never get rid of it.

John Krivine: (p. 107) I saw Poly Styrene at the Roxy and she was completely adorable. The freshness and vitality of these performers has never been reproduced.

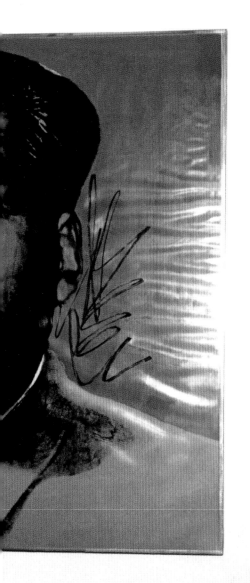

Caroline Coon and Paul Simonon (opposite)

Don Letts: Caroline Coon was one of the journalists that first picked up on Punk; John [Jonh] Ingham, [Tony] Parsons, [Vivien] Goldman, Janet Street-Porter. They were part of helping to break the thing.

Tracey O'Keefe and Debbie Juvenile
Generation X gig, December 1976 (p. 110 top)

Sharon Hayman (p. 110 bottom)

Susan Carrington (p. 111)

Andy Czezowski (p. 112)

Don Letts: Nuff respect to Andrew Czezowski. He picked up on the whole vibe of Punk; the fact that these kids have got attitude, and they've got sound but they've got no place to play. He provided the third vital ingredient in any good movement – the place, the base, the head-quarters for like minded people to come together and out of that togetherness came more ideas. Roxy was a major part of the scene.

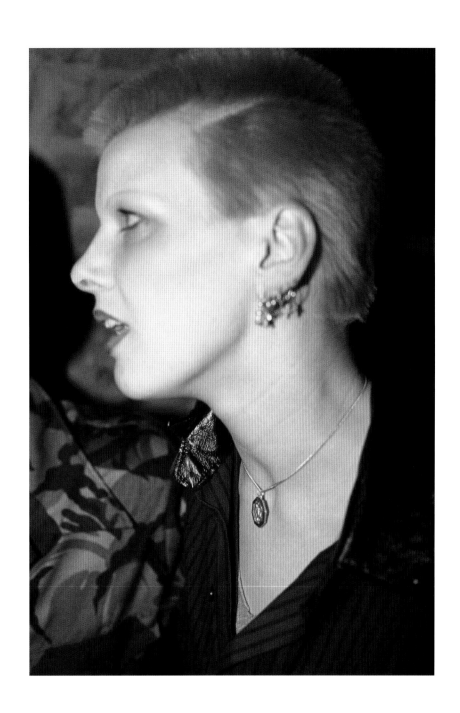

The Bromley Contingent (p. 114 – 121)

Debbie Juvenile (p. 114)

Soo Catwoman (p. 115)

Jeannette Lee and Hilde with members of the Bromley Contingent – Electric Circus, Manchester (p. 116)

Simon Barker, Billy Idol, Steven Severin, Siouxsie Sioux, Debbie Juvenile – Acme Attractions, November 1976

(p. 121 clockwise from top left)

John Krivine: The true fashionados, the elegant, stylish Punks were the Bromley Contingent and they were all loyal to Vivienne [Westwood].

Steven Severin: We got our clothes mainly from jumble sales. We augmented our look with the odd piece from SEX that we could afford. It wasn't cheap! We would all swap items, mix and match as well, just to keep things fresh.

Jeannette Lee: (p. 116) The leather jacket that I am wearing in this picture has got so much history. I bought it from Chrissie Hynde and then Joe Strummer borrowed it from me and I borrowed his jacket that was covered in zips. And then one night he came to my place in Forest Hill and said, `I need my jacket, we've got a band meeting. I can't turn up in a leather jacket´.

The Clash at the ICA – November 1976 (p. 122–125)

Paul Cook, Paul Simonon, John Ingham, Caroline Coon and Soo Catwoman (opposite, clockwise from top left)

Joe Strummer / Sarah Hall, Paul Simonon, Joe Strummer / Esther Dior and Joe Strummer

(above from left to right)

John Simon Ritchie later known as Sid Vicious (p. 125)

Don Letts: (p. 125) It's a sad story really, Sid was never vicious – he was the antithesis.

MUSIC

One of the most memorable and lasting impacts of Punk was its music. But exposure was hard-won: many Punk musicians were self-taught, and there were no recordings or albums initially. You relied on live music at gigs, advertised through word of mouth or via posters, flyers, badges and fanzines.

And yet, until the Roxy opened at the end of 1976, there were no dedicated venues in London to see Punk bands, while many local councils cancelled or banned appearances due to the movement's negative reputation. The wild, unruly behaviour and the public swearing of bands like the Sex Pistols did not fit in with conservative Britain. However, the exciting cocktail of energy, misbehaving and provocation was seductive to British youth, and bands were supported by a fiercely loyal fan base.

I went to the Roxy and experienced the music, but I was more interested in Punk's flamboyance and visual inventiveness. Other photographers also took pictures at the gigs, but it was rarer to capture them in the context of London at the time, which I aimed to do.

Subway Sect – Rehearsal Rehearsals, Chalk Farm,
December 1976 (p. 129 – 135)
Paul Myers, Rob Symmons, Paul Packham, Vic Godard
(p. 129 from left to right)

Sheila Rock: The band pose in this quirky almost Diane
Arbus kind of way.

Rob Symmons: They're the only public photographs
of us that exist from that time because we wouldn't
have any photographs taken. When you [Sheila Rock]
rang the door bell (that little black door at the side of
Rehearsal Rehearsals) you asked for The Clash and were
disappointed they were not there, didn't believe us, and
came in to see. To save a wasted trip, you reluctantly
photographed us. After we told Bernie [Rhodes] you had
come to the studio one evening and taken our pictures,
he was cross. I remember his exact words: 'When the
cat's away the mice will play'.

Rob Symmons: We were originally rehearsing in the King's Road. Malcolm [McLaren] came to see us. We used to go and see the Sex Pistols in the early days when there weren't many people there so he knew us. He wanted us to play the 100 Club Punk Special and when he saw us he realised that we couldn't play – we just made a right racket, a cacophonous caterwauling.

Malcolm got the rehearsal studio owner to open up early in the morning to let us in. We could hear him through the door saying, 'This group are going to be massive. You've got to help them out, they've got no money. You should get in early in the morning because it's going to make your place famous.' And true to his word, he got the bloke to open up early morning so we could rehearse all day. But Malcolm came to see us again that night and we still weren't good enough. We had no money for any more rehearsals so he said to Bernie [Rhodes], 'Can they use your place?' So we rehearsed over at Rehearsal Rehearsals all weekend before the Punk Special.

We went down there a lot and rehearsed non-stop, every day except for when The Clash used it. We also used to go to the subway under Hammersmith Broadway on Wednesday afternoons when it was games at school. We'd take our guitars with us and busk to help us get enough confidence to play live. We were the Sect.

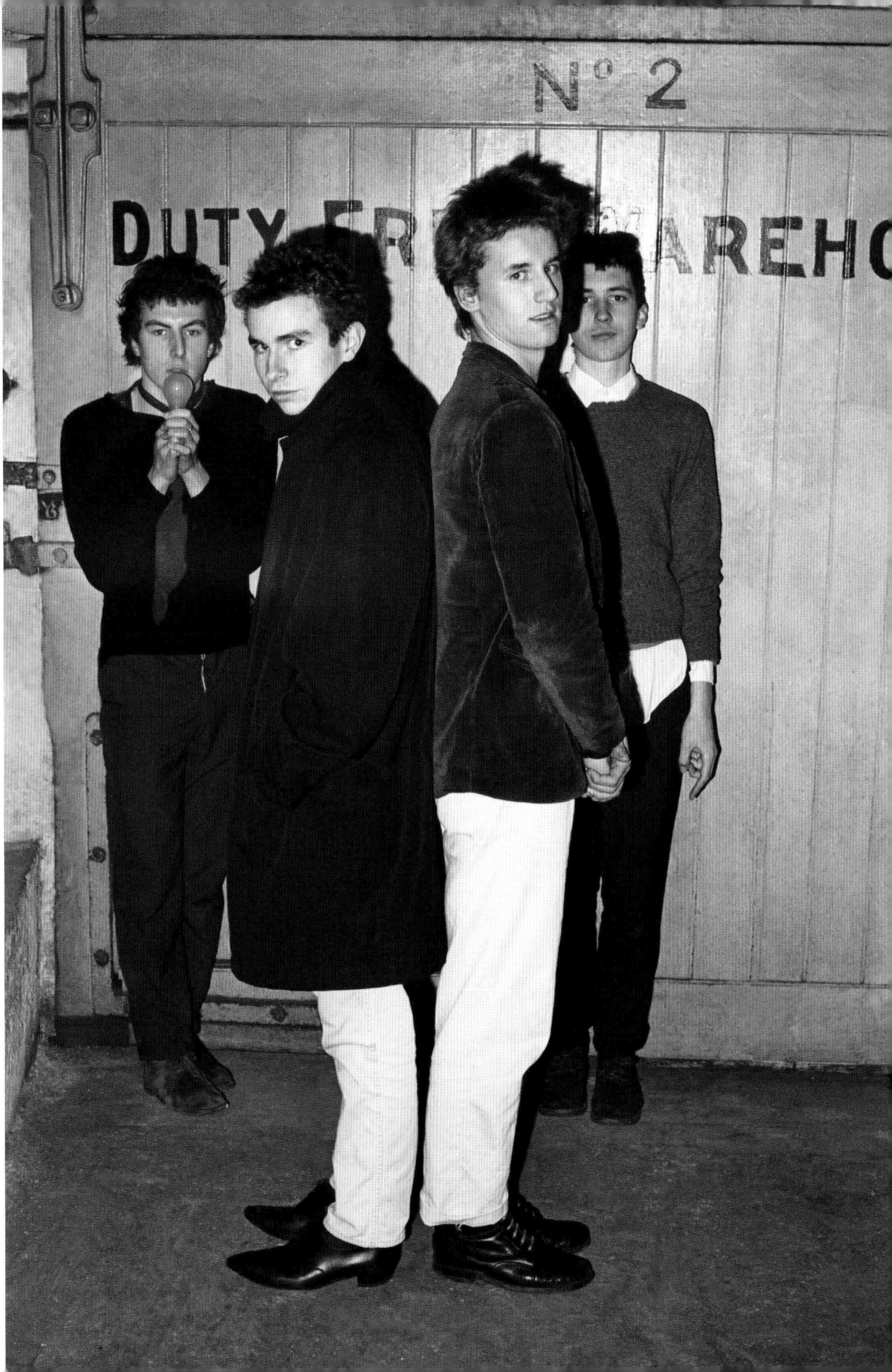
N° 2
DUTY

The Moors Murderers – The Arches, Waterloo, London, November 1977 (p. 136 – 143)

Steve Strange (p. 136 – 137)

Unknown, Steve Strange, John (Photons), unknown, Jane Suck and Chrissie Hynde

(p. 138 – 139 from left to right)

Lloyd Johnson: Steve Strange used to come and sit in my place when he came up from Newport. They were all looking for the scene and it hadn't developed yet.

Chrissie Hynde: I met Steve Strange at the Roxy. He came up to me and asked, 'Can you play?'. He had a lot of songs, well-written ones, about criminals, and sang one a cappella to me about Ian Brady. Steve had interest from a record company and needed to look like he'd got a band. I was keeping a low profile because I was writing for the *NME* and didn't want to be known. He said, 'No one will know it's you because we will all be wearing bin liners.' I was delighted just to play guitar in the background. We all had fake names – mine was Christine Hindley. When a reporter from *Sounds* reviewed our gig, they put our real names. The press jumped on the story because of the actual Moors Murderers. I was horrified. I got nailed because I already had a name as I was writing for the *NME*. I accidentally sabotaged the band. Their legacy was bigger than the band was.

Eater – Leee Black Childers' apartment, Islington
December 1976 (p. 144 –149)

Ian Woodcock, Brian Chevette, Andy Blade and Dee Generate
(p. 144 – 145 from left to right)

Don Letts: Eater – filmed them down at the Roxy once.
They decided to chop up a pig's head in the middle of
their performance as their pièce de résistance.

Dee Generate – he's a social worker now.

Andy Blade: The excitement of the time, what was
happening all around us, and to us, is captured perfectly by this handful of shots – you can see it in our
eyes. It helped that we liked Sheila too. I could sense in
her a slight nervousness in what she was doing, and
because I knew that feeling so well, it made me feel
completely comfortable.

Eater was a passage of rites. A bit of growing up done
in a very unusual way. Whilst our friends were coming
up to their exams, and school was their life, we were
gigging and recording, meeting pop stars, and getting
paid for it!

Sid used to wear that T-shirt I've got on (p. 149). He
threw it at me at a gig and I brought it home. Everyone
thought it was just a rag but my mum incorporated more
rips, the zip and letters with the remains.

PARENTS
WARNED
OVER GLUE
SNIFFING

The Clash – December 1976 and 1977 (p. 150 – 169)

Paul Simonon, Topper Headon, Mick Jones and Joe Strummer

(p. 162 – 163 from left to right)

Sheila Rock: (p. 153) Bernie [Rhodes] used this image for their first Roxy gig on the 1st January, 1977. I was completely chuffed to have a band poster.

Don Letts: The Clash's body of work gave Punk rock a depth and gravitas beyond guitars and mohawks.

Chris Salewicz: The Clash's music is more like satire – drawing attention to monsters.

Paul Simonon: Bernie [Rhodes] said, 'Write about things that affect you', and just left it to you to do the work. Same as with the clothing – he would come up with a quip like: 'Why is an audience going to listen to a band if the audience is better dressed than the band?', and you'd go away to think about it.

Jon Savage: The Clash's paint-splattered Jackson Pollock shirts looked good and they were something kids could do themselves which I thought was very important.

Glen Matlock: I found a bit of board that I did the first Jackson Pollock trousers on. A white board with a trouser shape on it. When The Clash turned up for the Anarchy tour they all had spray-painted clothes which they never had 'til then. I was gobsmacked.

Paul Simonon: I remember seeing the Pistols in Denmark Street and the band were in casuals. John [Lydon] was wearing baggy second-hand trousers and Paul [Cook] and Steve [Jones] were in Levi jeans. I noticed Glen's trousers and thought he was sporting a paisley-patterned print. I did for a brief moment consider: 'Why is Glen wearing Laura Ashley trousers?' On closer inspection it was paint but not well-defined. It is true that Glen's hand-painted trousers were an inspiration. I took the visual suggestion and exaggerated it! Rauschenberg and Jackson Pollock were the only contemporary artists that I admired while at art college in the mid-Seventies and the early days of The Clash. I utilised the influences of Robert Rauschenberg, Jackson Pollock and Glen Matlock!

Paul Simonon: (p. 161) Mick [Jones] was living with his nan so we'd always put the nan backdrop behind him. Having the bomber and the nan was quite a contrast. In some ways, one negates the other.

Chris Salewicz: It was fantastic on the White Riot tour when The Clash played at The Rainbow. The seats were ripped up and passed onto the front of the stage. They were playing behind a wall – the seats were gradually getting higher.

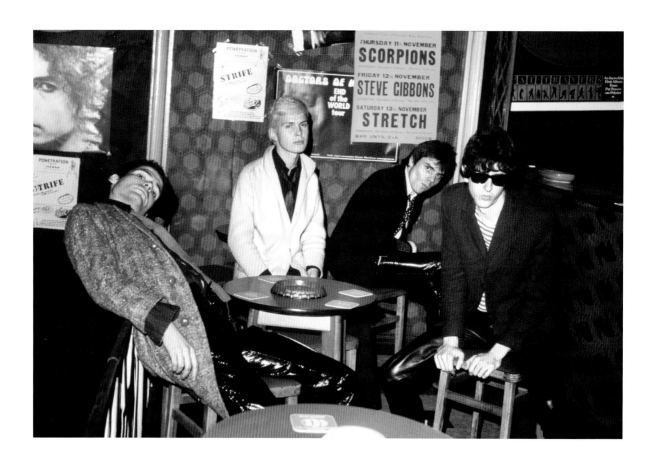

Chelsea – Manchester, 1976 (p. 170 – 171)
John Towe, Billy Idol, Gene October and Tony James (p. 170 from left to right)
Generation X – 1977 (p. 172 – 183)
Bob 'Derwood' Andrews, Tony James, John Towe, and Billy Idol (p. 172 – 173 from left to right)

Tony James: John Krivine ran some adverts in *Melody Maker* and those adverts trawled quite a lot of people like Marco [Pirroni], me and Bill [Billy Idol] who would turn up in Punk groups later.
John Krivine: I wanted a band. I found Tony and Bill. Bill was at Sussex University. They needed a singer. A boy with all the panache of Alex DeLarge [*A Clockwork Orange*] hung around the shop and reckoned he could sing. So, I bought some amplifiers and speakers, named this creation Chelsea and rechristened the singer Gene October. Bill and Tony didn't like Gene, there was an October revolution and I got fired.
Tony James: Generation X was my perfect group: a star singer, a guitar hero and an explosive rhythm section. In 1977, we felt invincible, that we could achieve anything. Was that just the confidence of youth or a perfect moment in time?

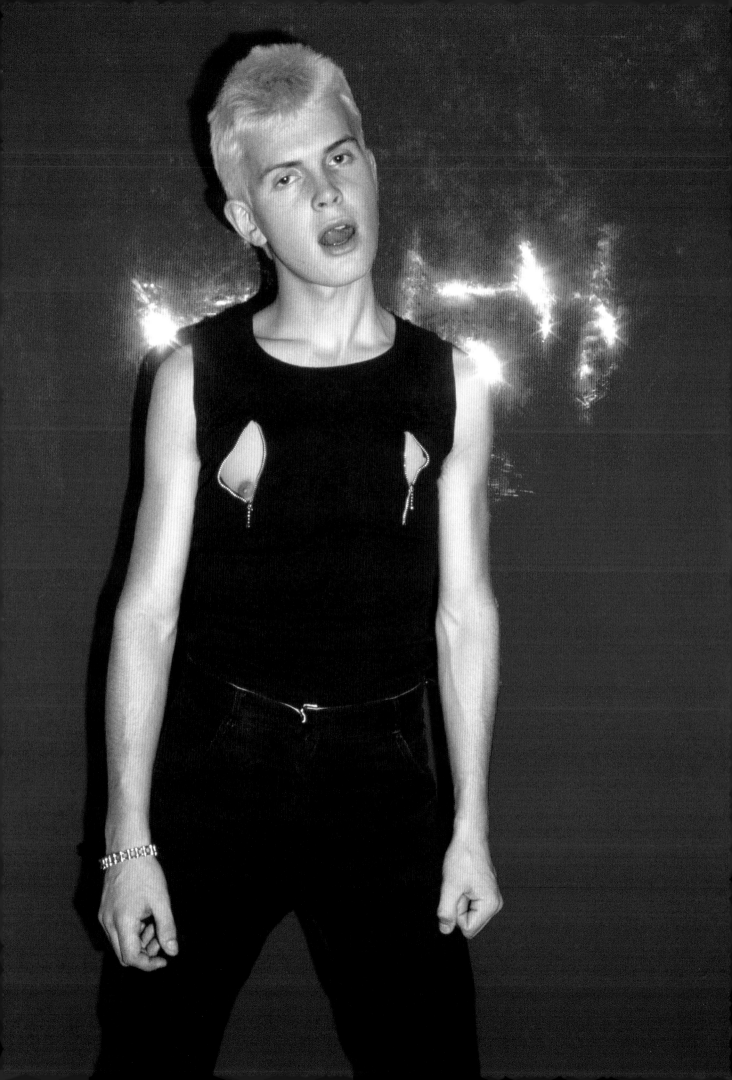

Mark Laff, Tony James, Billy Idol and Bob 'Derwood' Andrews – Embankment, London (from left to right)

Tony James: We played the first gig at the Roxy – in fact, we built the stage, me and Derwood. We had to cut his long hair the day we played that Roxy gig. In those days, cutting your hair and wearing the right jacket were majorly important things.

The Buzzcocks – November 1977 (p. 184 – 191)
Pete Shelley, Steve Garvey, Steve Diggle and John Maher
(p. 186 – 187 from left to right)

Glen Matlock: At their first gig they ended the set with `Boredom´ which went on and on and on and on and on.
Paul Simonon: We did a couple of shows with the Buzzcocks and we used to go on stage with the Jackson Pollock shirts. One time they did a show with us and they went on with Mondrian shirts. It was great!
Don Letts: The Buzzcocks brought some emotion into Punk rock. Love songs. Radical. And they were great live. Great songs, catchy songs. Famously put out the first DIY Punk rock single. They were a major factor in the independent scene springing up.

Siouxsie and the Banshees – 1976 (p. 194 – 197)

Jon Savage: Siouxsie – she was like a dominatrix.
Steven Severin: We were the vanguard and I don't think we were prepared for the whole thing to just explode.

The Damned – November 1976 (p. 198 – 209)
Brian James, Rat Scabies, Dave Vanian and Captain Sensible
(p. 200 – 201 from left to right)

Chrissie Hynde: Malcolm [McLaren] wanted to start a band called Masters of the Backside. He got a drummer called Chris Miller, Ray Burns, two singers called Dave – Dave White and Dave Zero and me as the guitar player. I was to stand in the back and pretend to be a boy. We worked out a few songs then Malcolm, Vivienne [Westwood] and Little Helen [Wellington-Lloyd] came to see us rehearse at a church hall. Malcolm was pleased but two days later Ray Burns changed his name to Captain Sensible, Dave Zero to Dave Vanian and they fucked off with Chris [Rat Scabies] to become The Damned.

Chris Salewicz: Fantastically theatrical and quite unique and completely separate from everyone else really. It was a fantastic show.

Don Letts: They rocked the house; they would rock the Roxy more than any other band and played there more regularly than anyone else.

The Cortinas – Roundhouse, June 1977 (p. 216 – 217)
Nick Sheppard, Mike Fewings [hidden], Jeremy Valentine, Daniel Swann and Dexter Dalwood [out of picture]
(from left to right)

Jon Savage: The Cortinas' bassist Dexter Dalwood is now a major artist and was shortlisted for the Turner Prize a couple of years ago.

The Jam – November 1977 to June 1979 (p. 218 – 229)
Bruce Foxton, Rick Buckler and Paul Weller
(p. 218 from left to right)

Paul Simonon: With The Jam and The Stranglers, Punk was starting to splinter into different genres.

Tony James: Punks were quite sneery about The Jam because of the blazers and suits, even though Weller was clearly really great.

Glen Matlock: Weller asked me to join them. They said, 'Will you wear a suit?', I said, 'Yeah', and they said, 'What, like ours', and I said, 'From Carnaby Cavern?', and they said, 'Yeah', and I said, 'You must be fucking joking' and that was the end of it.

Chris Salewicz: The Jam were subjected to criticism over their punk credentials – they were not part of punk's inner sanctum. Joe Strummer even criticised them in his masterpiece '(White Man) In Hammersmith Palais'; identifying The Jam by their 'Burton suits', he dismissed them as a new group 'not concerned with what there is to be learned'. This, ultimately, may have led to audiences identifying with them as underdogs.

Of all the groups that emerged from the 1977 cultural revolution, The Jam were the only one to come near to rivalling the success of The Clash. The first month of 1977 they are doing the Roxy, July they are selling out Hammersmith Odeon on their own – 4,000 people. Extraordinary.

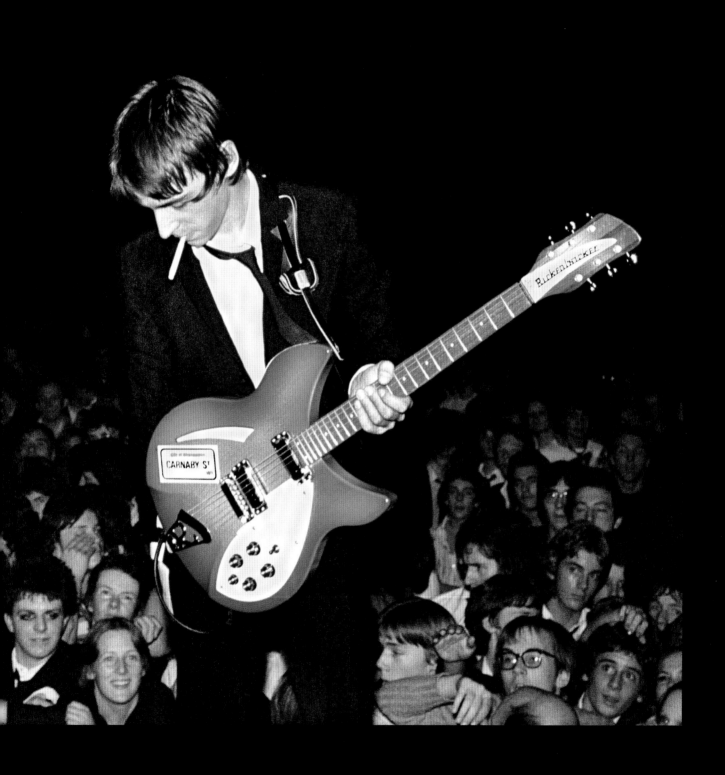

The Stranglers – Brighton, June 1977 (p. 230 – 233)

Jean-Jacques Burnel, Hugh Cornwell, Jet Black and Dave Greenfield (p. 230 from left to right)

Jeannette Lee: At the time, The Stranglers didn't feel like they were part of it or like they fitted in but with the passing of time, they do fit in.

Paul Simonon: The Stranglers – they were an entity in their own right as a band. I suppose because of their name at the time, the press assumed they were a Punk band so they got pulled into it. Strangely enough that jumper (p. 232) looks very similar to one I had.

INFLUENCE

Despite its long-lasting impact, the Punk era was quite short. Within a few years, Punk became increasingly commercial and broke up into a series of subcultures, including Goth, Two-Tone, Rockabilly, New Wave and New Romantics. Most of them had foundations in Punk.

As the Seventies and Punk drew to an end and my career as a photographer grew, I went to work for publications like *The Face* magazine. *The Face* was groundbreaking, innovative and radical in its design. It soon set a new tone for magazine publishing and influenced the music and fashion of the Eighties.

My photographs and this book record a key time in Punk's trajectory, from creative cultural upheaval to tabloid spectacle. Like the Punks themselves, I was making it up as I went along. Often, I'd go to the photo lab praying the photos would come out. I wasn't thinking about posterity. I was just going with the flow and enjoying this transformative time.

Johnsons The Modern Outfitters – 1979

Lloyd Johnson
406 KING'S ROAD, LONDON, SW3

Chris Salewicz: This shop was phenomenal. It was a real statement when it opened and the shop in Kensington Market was running at the same time. I remember Lloyd doing all those single-breasted, needlecord suits with lapels and Andy Warhol print shirts. It was quite revolutionary and on The Clash On Parole tour, Paul [Simonon] had a single-breasted, thin lapel, mohair-like suit.

Lloyd Johnson: At first I had all these '60s newspapers with the Mods and Rockers stuck on the wall. I varnished them so it looked like it was nicotine-stained. The whole décor was rough brick walls with fake flowers – anything I found in the dustbin.

Glen Matlock: I had the very first 2 Tone suit. Lloyd had told me these were coming in so I was there at 9.30 in the morning, unloaded the car, tried them on and I got this really good silver tonic suit. But the whole arse got ripped out of it. The next day I wore it when we did the Old Grey Whistle Test so I had to keep my front to the camera.

Lloyd Johnson: That's Peter [Boutwood] putting the collars up. I had to go round putting them back down.

World's End – 1982 (p. 247)
Vivienne Westwood – 1980 (p. 248 – 249)
430 KING'S ROAD, LONDON, SW3

John Krivine: Vivienne's clothing was inspirational.
Don Letts: I became very friendly with Vivienne. We went out one night and I had on my electric blue zoot suit and she had on a see-through rubber leotard made of stuff that looked like condoms. We cut a fine form that night, let me tell you.

Robot – 1980 (p. 250 – 253)
37 FLORAL STREET, LONDON, WC2E 9DJ

Lloyd Johnson: We ordered some black leather shoes from George Cox. The almond-toed '50s ones with stitching round the toes and purple, suede uppers. The shop was opening, they hadn't come. We had waited six months for these shoes to arrive and I said we can't wait any longer. I cancelled the order. Three weeks later those shoes were delivered to Mike [McManus] and Dave's [Fortune] place in Beaufort Market. That place became Robot.

Siouxsie and the Banshees – February 1979

(p. 254 – 261)

Steven Severin, John McKay, Siouxsie Sioux and Kenny Morris

(from left to right p. 257)

Steven Severin: The most important aspects of Punk:
Propulsion. Action. Autonomy. Destiny.

The Cure — 1978 (p. 263 – 265)

Michael Dempsey, Lol Tolhurst and Robert Smith

(from left to right p. 263)

Sheila Rock: This 'Robot shoes and Johnsons leather jacket' look has become an archetypal rock and roll look.

John Lydon – 1980 (p. 267 – 271, 276 – 279)
Public Image Limited – 1980 (p. 272 – 275)
Keith Levene, Jah Wobble and John Lydon
(from left to right p. 275)

Don Letts: When the Sex Pistols broke up, John was looking to escape the paparazzi. He went to Jamaica with Richard Branson to start a reggae label called Frontline. I'm John's mate, I'm black and he figures I must know what's what and invites me to go with him. Funnily enough, the closest I'd ever been to Jamaica was watching The Harder They Come in Brixton.

Richard Branson booked a whole floor of the Sheraton and over the next three or four weeks it was like an exodus of musicians. Everyone was trying to get a deal so we sat there surrounded by these mythical names we'd only seen on 45s. Probably the most amazing trip of my life.

Paul Simonon: Bernie [Rhodes] got John to be the singer in the Pistols. They had met in the street when Malcolm [McLaren] was in New York and Bernie was getting the Pistols together. I think that's amusing because he had tried to get me to sing for them too. John and I had that connection.

Jeannette Lee: Gunter Grove – that reminds me of endless nights not going to sleep, listening to music all night long. It was the beginning of what I do now.

Jah Wobble: PIL was exhilarating. Punk had become very tiresome. Suddenly I was in a situation where I could express myself and play bass. I knew Punk had opened a big window of opportunity for me.

PUBLIC IMAGE LTD

THE METAL
PUBLIC

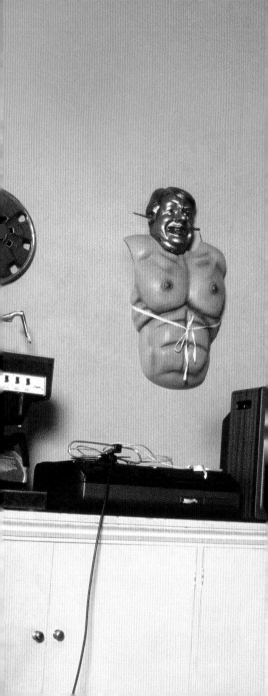

LEGACY

Looking back, it is clear that Punk came out of a terrible economic situation and that many young people in Britain embraced its early Deconstructivist vision. It was a reaction against conservative ideas and music that was either formulaic or, like progressive rock, full of instrumentation and complicated compositional techniques.

America had its own Punk style and music, which manifested in an arty way. It came out of New York City and evolved out of the Velvet Underground and Andy Warhol's factory scene. It was middle class and arts school whereas British Punk was more political, anarchistic and certainly more visually adventurous.

I was fortunate to have been on the King's Road and to have met some of the early Punk heroes. Don Letts, now a celebrated DJ and filmmaker, introduced me to virtually everyone important on the small scene. We grouped together because we shared a need to explore our inner passions. We had no idea that Punk was going to be so big or have such a lasting impact, but often when you are in the wave you can't see its shape or strength.

Haute Couture and Goth Punk

KING'S CROSS, LONDON

Sheila Rock: Goth subculture emerged on the streets during the early 1980s, as an off shoot of Post-Punk. The style of dress drew on Punk and New Romantic fashion and was typically black and mysterious. Goth often borrowed from the Victorian era.

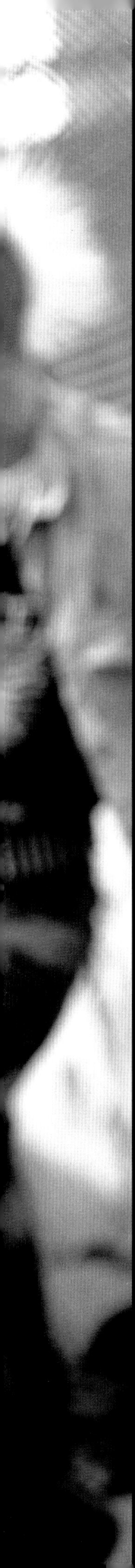

Moda magazine shoot
Amanda Cazelet (p. 284)
WEST LONDON

Sheila Rock: For a movement that lasted for a very short time in its purest form, Punk has had a remarkably long legacy. Haute couture is still borrowing from Punk. From leather and ripped-up clothes, to dress slits held together with safety pins, combined with modified Mohawk hairstyles, its influence on fashion lives on.

The commercialism of Punk
All clothes featured are from Boy, King's Road, London

Sheila Rock: The early 1980s saw Punk veer from a protest movement expressing the discontent of the UK youth into high-street commercialism. Bright and cheaply made clothes – knocking off the darker, more creative originals – became touted in the tabloids and widely available in shops. That legacy continues today.

Interviewees

Andy Blade – musician, Eater / Chrissie Hynde – musician, Moors Murderers, The Pretenders / John Krivine – fashion entrepreneur, owner of Acme and Boy / Tony James – Chelsea, Generation X / Lloyd Johnson – fashion designer, entrepreneur and owner of Johnsons The Modern Outfitters / Jeannette Lee – Acme, PIL manager / Don Letts – Acme, Roxy DJ, filmmaker / Glen Matlock – musician, Sex Pistols / Chris Salewicz – writer and journalist / Jon Savage – writer and journalist / Steven Severin – musician, Siouxsie and the Banshees / Paul Simonon – musician, The Clash / Rob Symmons – musician, Subway Sect / Jah Wobble – musician, PIL.

Our thanks to

All our interviewees for their help and kindness.

Also to Agnès B., Sébastien Ruiz and Stéphane Lapierre at Agnès B. / David Barraclough / Dave Brolan / Cally / Nathalie Cicurel / Andrew Krivine / Rudi Esch / Colin Fallows / Lora Findlay / Imogen Gordon Clark / Martin Green / Jordan / Michael Kasparis and Nina Hervé at Rough Trade / James Lawler / Lincoln Norton / Mark Paytress / Jem Rigby / Jane Shepherd / Carl Williams.

Special thanks to Sarah Simonon and Fabrice Couillerot for *Punk+*.

Sheila Rock

Sheila Rock is a professional photographer living in London. In addition to being featured in numerous books, magazines and private commissions, her work is housed in the permanent collection of the National Portrait Gallery, London. The photo-journalistic images of Punk in this book were taken in the early stages of her career. She continued to capture the changes in youth culture and music for over a decade while working with magazines such as *The Face*. She is currently working on a number of fine art projects and exhibits internationally. *Punk+* was her second book.

www.sheilarock.com